IMAGES
of America

BASEBALL
IN DETROIT
1886–1968

IMAGES

of America

BASEBALL
IN DETROIT
1886–1968

David Lee Poremba

ARCADIA
PUBLISHING

ISBN 978-1-5316-6037-6

Published by Arcadia Publishing
Charleston, South Carolina

Library of Congress Catalog Card Number: 98-88056

For all general information contact Arcadia Publishing at:
Telephone 843-853-2070
Fax 843-853-0044
E-mail sales@arcadiapublishing.com
For customer service and orders:
Toll-Free 1-888-313-2665

Visit us on the Internet at www.arcadiapublishing.com

*To Tiger fans everywhere,
especially Harold, Teresa, Joseph, and Brian.*

CONTENTS

ACKNOWLEDGMENTS

Grateful acknowledgment is made to Mr. Richard Bak for the use of some of the photographs seen here, taken from his extensive collection.

The majority of the pictures are from the Ernie Harwell Sports Collection of the Burton Historical Collection at the Detroit Public Library. Over 30 years ago, Mr. Harwell donated his vast personal collection of sports history to the library for the use and enjoyment of the people of the city of Detroit. For that kindness, we are all eternally grateful.

INTRODUCTION

The first baseball game to take place in Detroit between two organized teams was probably the game played on August 8, 1859, between the Early Risers and the Detroits, two teams made up of merchants and store clerks. The Early Risers were so named because they took their practice at 4:00 a.m., before the workday started. The Detroits' roster consisted of those gentlemen who could afford to practice at any time. The two teams squared off at 2:30 p.m. at the Cass Farm, the Risers getting clobbered 59 to 12.

Baseball continued to be played by, and was considered, a gentlemen's sport through the late 1800s. The American Civil War helped spread the popularity of the game and opened up its participation to all enthusiasts. By the 1870s, professionalism had entered the sport, and local organizers were willing to bet that Detroiters would become enthusiastic spectators.

Detroit's first group of professional baseball players was organized in the spring of 1879 and played their games at Recreation Park, on the city's east side, where Grace Hospital now stands. In 1881, Detroit was awarded a franchise in the National League, which was seeking a western city to replace the Cincinnati club. The mayor of Detroit, William G. Thompson, and his backers, paid $20,000 for the franchise and had arranged for the games to be played at Recreation Park. The team was nicknamed the Wolverines and prepared to take the field dressed in red-trimmed, light gray uniforms with cardinal red belts and stockings.

The team consistently lost more games than they won, never finishing higher than fourth place during their first five seasons. After several ownership changes, Frederick Stearnes took control and purchased the "Big Four" infield from Buffalo. This led to Detroit's only pre-1900 World Championship in 1887.

After the following season, the club was sold off piecemeal, and the city was without a major league team for several years.

Over the winter of 1893–1894, Ban Johnson visited the city to see if he would include it in his reorganized Western League. The talks proved to be successful, and Detroit has had a major league team representing it from that time on.

In 1901, Johnson claimed that his league was of major league quality, and he renamed it the American League, survived a recognition battle with the National League, and cleaned up the image of the game. The Detroit Tigers are charter members of that league, which is fast approaching its centennial.

The Detroit Tigers have given generations of Detroit fans more than their fair share of thrills and disappointments. From the three-time pennant winners of this century's first decade, down to the last real championship team of 1968, Detroiters have flocked to see their team play, win or lose. The fact that they have played at the same intersection of town for just over a century is a tribute to the pride and loyalty that the team and the fans have shown each other. No other baseball franchise has such a close relationship with its constituency.

One

THE 1880S AND 1890S

THE 1886 DETROIT WOLVERINES. Pictured from left to right are as follows: (front row) Charles Getzein, Larry Twitchell, Manager William H. Watkins, Hardie Richardson, and Charles Bennett; (middle row) Deacon White, Elmer Sutcliff, Dan Brouthers, Harry Gruber, Sam Thompson, Charles Ganzel, and Charles Baldwin; (back row) Jack Rowe, Pete Conway, Ned Hanlon, and Eb Beatin. Joining the National League in 1881 as a replacement for the Cincinnati team, the Wolverines suffered through some dismal seasons. In 1885, Detroit bought the entire Buffalo team for $7,000 in order to acquire four players known as the "Big Four" (Brouthers, Richardson, Rowe, and White). The team went from dead last in 1884 to a second place finish in 1886 with an 87-36 record, 2 1/2 games behind the Chicago White Stockings.

DAN BROUTHERS. One of baseball's 19th-century superstars, Dan won the league's batting championship five times. He won his first in 1882 with a .368 average and repeated the next season by batting .374. Brouthers came to Detroit from Buffalo in 1886 and hit .370. Brouthers was large for his era at 6 feet, 2 inches and 205 pounds.

DAN BROUTHERS. Brouthers was a capable fielder at first base—barehanded as all ballplayers of the period were—but his best contributions were at the plate. On September 10, 1886, he blasted three home runs, a double, and a single for 15 total bases. After retirement, John McGraw placed him in charge of the Polo Grounds press gate.

CHARLIE BENNETT. One of the fan favorites in Detroit was the sturdy catcher, Charlie Bennett. He entered the National League in 1878 with Milwaukee and then Worcester before coming to the team in 1881. He stayed through the 1887 season and was dealt to the Boston Beaneaters. His career ended when he lost both legs in a train accident in 1894. He was an outstanding defensive catcher and became the first one to wear a chest protector in 1886. Charlie eventually returned to Detroit and opened a business. The crippled catcher caught the ceremonial first pitch at every home opener from 1895 to 1926. He died just weeks before the 1927 season started.

JACK ROWE. Nattily attired in the fashion of the day, Rowe was part of the "Big Four" of Buffalo who came to Detroit in 1885. Jack moved from catcher to shortstop that season, and in 1887 scored a career high 135 runs and posted a .318 batting average. He hardly ever struck out (only 177 times in 4,386 at-bats) and went the entire 1882 season without striking out.

HARDY RICHARDSON. "Old True Blue" played every position on the field at one time or another, but was best known as one of the greatest second basemen of the 19th century. A part of the "Big Four," Richardson hit .328 with 11 home runs and 94 runs batted in during the 1887 championship season.

12

FRED DUNLAP. "Sure Shot" Dunlap, at various times in his career, led National League second basemen in all fielding categories and twice hit over .300. Coming to the Detroits in time for the 1886 season, he hit .286 for the year with four home runs. In 1887, he hit .265 with a hefty .441 slugging average.

CHARLES BUSTED BALDWIN. "Lady" Baldwin came to Detroit from Milwaukee in time for the 1885 season, when he won 11 and lost 9. In 1886, he led the league in shutouts with 7 and tied for the lead in wins with 42. He got his nickname from his teammates because he didn't drink, smoke, or curse.

SAM THOMPSON. "Big Sam" was a 6-foot, 2-inch, 207-pound carpenter who began playing professional baseball in 1884. He was acquired by Detroit the following year and hit for a .303 average. In 1887, he led the league with 545 at-bats, 203 hits, 23 triples, 166 RBIs (the highest 19th-century RBI total), and a .372 batting average. He hit 128 home runs in the dead-ball era.

WILLIAM SHINDLE. Bill Shindle was born during the Civil War and came to the Detroit team at the ripe old age of 22 as a utility player. He played seven games at shortstop in 1885 and played back-up third base behind Deacon White for 21 games in 1887.

14

HENRY WEIDMAN. "Stump" Weidman was a right-handed pitcher who came to Detroit from the Buffalo club in 1881. He remained in Detroit through the 1885 season, was dealt to Kansas City for a year, then returned to Detroit in time for the world championship. Stump went 13-7 in 1887, second best on the team. He also hit .207 in 82 at-bats.

THE NEW YORK GIANTS, 1888. This Giants team finished the 1887 season in fourth place, 10 1/2 games behind Detroit. They won 68 and lost 55 games and had such great stars and future hall-of-famers like Roger Connor, Montgomery Ward, Buck Ewing, Tim Keefe, and Mickey Welch.

THE PHILADELPHIA QUAKERS, 1888. The Quakers beat out the Chicago club for second place in 1887 and finished 3 1/2 games behind, winning 75 and losing 48 games. Their best performers were pitchers. Hurlers Dan Casey, Charles Ferguson, and Charles Bufinton each won 20 games, and Casey led the league with a 2.86 earned run average.

THE CHICAGO WHITE STOCKINGS, 1888. The incumbent champions of 1886 finished the 1887 season in third place, 6 1/2 games behind, winning 71 and losing 50 games. Led by their player/manager Cap Anson, who hit for a .347 average, the team rode the arm of John Clarkson, who single-handedly pitched them into third place with 38 wins.

16

ADRIAN C. ANSON. Cap Anson is widely regarded as the premiere batsman and leader of 19th-century baseball. He began his professional career in 1871 with the Rockford Forest Citys of the National Association. He was one of the first players signed when the National League was launched in 1876, going to the Chicago team. He had a .352 lifetime batting average over 22 years.

ALBERT GOODWILL SPALDING. Another of baseball's premier pioneers, Spalding was a pitcher for the Boston Red Stockings in 1871 and retired from playing in 1877 to devote himself to his sporting goods store. From 1882 to 1891, he served as president of the Chicago team. He was baseball's first 20-game winner.

RECREATION PARK. An overflow crowd at John R. and Brush watch the Detroit Wolverines battle the defending champion White Stockings, led by the immortal Cap Anson. Notice the rather large number of horses and carriages in the deepest part of center field, providing no end of distractions for both teams.

CHAMPIONS OF THE LEAGUE, 1887. In a promotional piece that was evidently issued after the first of the new year, the starting lineup of the Detroits appear with their manager, Bill Watkins. With the acquisition of the "Big Four" from Buffalo, Detroit went from last in 1885 to a close second in 1886, and finally became the best in the league.

18

WORLD SERIES CONTENDERS, 1887. In order to make up for small gate receipts during the regular season, Detroit owner Frederick Strearnes challenged the St. Louis Browns, champions of the American Association, to a 15-game World Series, played in all major-league cities. The two teams traveled in a special train of parlor cars and employed the then-novel idea of using two umpires.

THE ST. LOUIS BROWNS, 1887. Led by their captain, Charley Comiskey, the Browns won four consecutive American Association (considered a major league) pennants. After splitting the first two games in St. Louis, the Wolverines won the third contest, 2-1 in 13 innings, on a Comiskey error. Detroit went on to win all but one of the next eight games to claim the World Championship.

THE WASHINGTON STATESMEN, 1880s. Based in the nation's capitol, this team would go through several nickname changes—first the Statesmen, then the Nationals, and finally the Senators. They were always a second-division team, but listed such stalwarts as Connie Mack at catcher (top row, middle) and "Dummy" Hoy, the deaf mute for whom the umpires developed signals (the raised arm became a called strike).

THE BROOKLYNS, 1880s. Playing in the American Association as the Bridegrooms, then in the National League as the Superbas and Tolley Dodgers and finally the Dodgers, this team always fielded a colorful group. In 1889, they unseated St. Louis on Oyster Burns's .304 average. In 1890, they won the National League flag after the great players revolt.

THE PHILADELPHIA PHILLIES, 1880s. The Phillies, as the Quakers were now known, were a hard-fighting team, always beating a sure club out of a finish. They sported big Ed Delahanty, one of five playing brothers, at second base, and, after Detroit folded, Sam Thompson in the outfield. Pitching for the Phillies was "Kid" Gleason, who later managed the Chicago "Black" Stockings of 1919.

THE CLEVELAND BLUES, 1889. The demise of the Detroit team at the end of the 1888 season saw the Blues jump en masse from the American Association to the National League, where they finished a distant sixth, 40 1/2 games off the mark. Jersey Bakely, their work-horse pitcher, finished the year with 25 wins and 33 losses.

THE CLEVELAND SPIDERS, 1890S. Although a perennial second-division team, the Spiders featured a young pitcher, Denton "Cy" Young (top row, middle), who would go on to post Hall-of-Fame statistics. Young would play for St. Louis in 1899 and 1900, when the Cleveland Spiders would post baseball's worst record of 20 wins and 134 losses, finishing 84 games out of first.

MAGNATES OF THE WESTERN LEAGUE, 1899. From left to right, they are as follows: (front row) T.J. Lofus, Louisville; M.J. O'Brien; Ban Johnson, president; J.H. Manning, Kansas City; George A. VanderBeck, Detroit; and C.H. Snulpaugh, Minnesota; (back row) R. Allen, Indianapolis; M.R. Killilea, Milwaukee; Connie Mack, Milwaukee; Charles A. Comiskey, St. Paul; and G.H. Schmelz. Ban Johnson organized this Midwestern association in 1894, with the hope of it ultimately becoming a major circuit.

THE DETROIT CREAMS, 1899. This is the first team to play at Michigan Avenue and Trumbull, starting in 1896. These players came to Detroit from a Los Angeles club of the California League. The roster contained some ex-National-League ball players, such as Sam Dungan, who batted .447 in the 1895 season. The team finished third in 1899.

THE COLUMBUS TEAM, 1899. Columbus opened the 1899 season in Detroit on April 27. They defeated the Tigers by a score of 4-2. They would never finish the season, retiring from the league in July. An entry from Grand Rapids would take their place and their record, finishing one game over .500. Hall-of-Fame pitcher Rube Waddell is standing second from the left.

THE MILWAUKEE TEAM, 1899. This Wisconsin team, owned in part by Connie Mack, finished the 1899 season in sixth place, winning 55 and losing 68. Outside of a couple of finely dressed pitchers, there is nothing much to say about them. As Ban Johnson pushed his league to major status, he would move teams east to challenge the nationals.

KANSAS CITY, 1899. This Kansas City team would finish the season tied for last place with the Buffalo entry. Each team won 53 and lost 70 games for a paltry .431 winning percentage. The Kansas City team would win five and lose two "Chicago" games. A "Chicago" game occurred when one side or the other failed to score a single run.

Umpires of the Western League, 1899. In an effort to keep the "rowdyism" that was a factor in the other leagues unpopularity out of his league, Ban Johnson insisted on the best behavior and performance of his men in blue. He also insisted that the players and managers respect them as well. This made for a more "genteel" game—one to please the ladies and attract more revenues to ballparks. Jack Sheridan was a National League umpire and went on to become a respected signal caller in the American League. On May 30, 1901, he was involved in the first American League forfeit involving Baltimore and Detroit, with the game going to the Tigers.

THE FANS, 1880s–1890s. Baseball fans, or "cranks" as they were called before the turn of the century, occupy these illegal bleacher seats just beyond the right-field wall at Bennett Park. The rickety, wooden structures looked unsafe, but never did collapse. Tiger owners attempted to get these stands torn down, mostly without success. They would hang down long canvas strips in front of them, creating the first "obstructed view" seats. It wasn't until well after 1900, when the owners bought up more land and remodeled the park, that the "wildcat stands" were finally disposed of.

Two

THE 1900S AND 1910S

THE 1900 DETROIT TIGERS. After molding the Western League into the strongest minor league in the country, Ban Johnson felt ready to play and compete with the National League as equals. When the Nationals trimmed their league from 12 teams to 8, Johnson moved quickly. He shifted a franchise to the vacated National League city of Cleveland, placed a team in the National League stronghold of Chicago, and renamed his group the American League. The league opened the 1900 season with eight teams in Buffalo, Chicago, Cleveland, Detroit, Indianapolis, Kansas City, Milwaukee, and Minneapolis.

THE 1901 TIGERS. Opening the season at Bennett Park on April 25 against the Milwaukee Brewers, the Tigers nearly disappointed the overflow crowd of ten thousand fans. Trailing 13-4 in the bottom of the ninth, Detroit rallied for ten runs to win the contest 14-13.

GEORGE TWEEDY STALLINGS. The "Miracle Man" managed the Tigers in their inaugural American League season to a third place finish with a .548 winning percentage. As a player-manager with Detroit, he hit the first home run at Michigan and Trumbull. He also managed the 1914 "Miracle" Boston Braves to a championship.

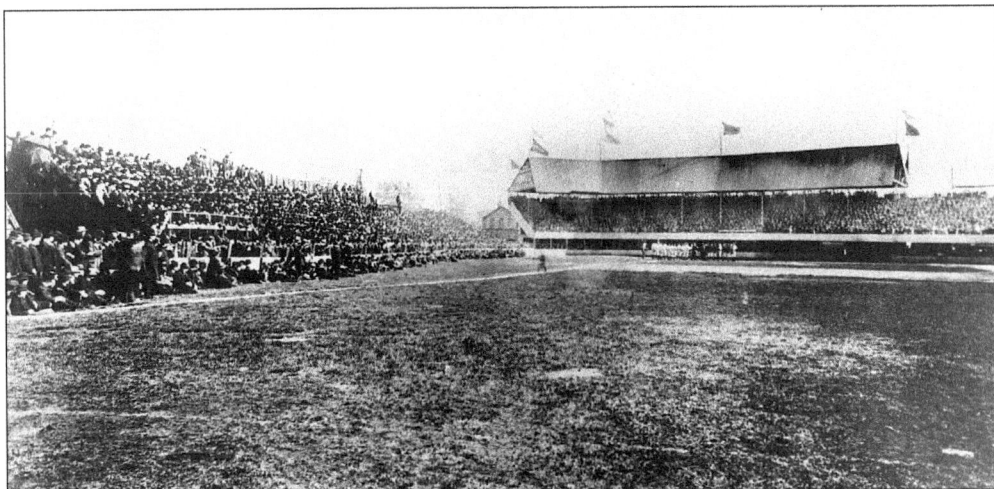

BENNETT PARK, 1901. Here is a view from right field looking toward home plate. Bennett Park, named after Detroit catcher Charlie Bennett, could comfortably accommodate overflow crowds in the perimeter of the outfield from right-center all the way around to left field. It was always decided before the game whether balls hit into the crowd were playable or ground-rule doubles. Note that home plate is in the present right-field corner.

THE 1903 TIGERS. The team that nearly moved to Pittsburgh during the winter of 1902 had to overcome the loss of their newly promoted player-manager Win Mercer, who took his own life. With new manager Ed Barrow, the Tigers began strongly but slid to sixth place by June. They finished fifth, 25 games out.

BENNETT PARK ACTION, 1903. In what is probably the first action-sports picture ever taken in Detroit, Wid Conroy of the New York Highlanders leaps high for a throw. The man on the right is umpire "Silk" O'Loughlin. The third base coach frantically waves the batter forward. (The photo was taken by William A. Kuenzel.)

THE 1905 TIGERS. Looking snappy, attired in their blue road uniforms, these Tigers were poised to be pennant contenders for several reasons. Under their fifth manager in five seasons, Bill Armour would lead them to a third place finish, over the .500 mark with a 79-74 record. They batted .243 as a team.

WILLIAM R. ARMOUR. Bill came over from the Cleveland club, after two seasons there, to manage the Tigers for the 1905 season. He is credited with finding and buying Ty Cobb for $750 from the Augusta, Georgia team while the Tigers were heading north to begin the season. He was replaced at the end of the 1906 season by Hugh Jennings.

THE TIGER DUGOUT, 1905. Bill Armour, sporting a brand straw boater, gives timely advice to rookie outfielder Ty Cobb. Acquired from the Augusta, Georgia club for $750 along with pitcher Ed Cicotte, Cobb would play his first game as a Tiger on August 30, against New York, at Bennett Park. He drove in two runs in the first inning with a double.

THE PLAYER OF THE CENTURY, TYRUS R. COBB. "Baseball is a red-blooded game for red-blooded men," the rookie declared. "Baseball is like war. It's no pink tea. Mollycoddlers had better stay out. It's a struggle for supremacy. A survival of the fittest." Hitting for an unnoticeable .240 average in his first year, Cobb would lead the American League in batting 12 times, 9 of them in a row from 1907 through 1916. He had a lifetime batting average of .367, the highest ever, and played 24 years in the league. Ty won the Triple Crown in 1909, when he led the league in home runs with 9, runs batted in with 115, and batting with a .377 average. Three times he hit over .400—in 1911 he hit .420, in 1912 he hit .410, and in 1922 he hit .401. He had 4,191 career hits, 892 stolen bases, and was the first player elected to the Hall of Fame in 1936.

AN OPENING DAY BLIZZARD, 1911. Davy Jones stands in against the Chicago White Sox in a blizzard of snow on April 16, 1911. That is Billy Sullivan behind the plate at catcher, who excelled in all aspects of catching. Ty Cobb called him the best catcher "to ever wear leather." His son, Billy Jr., caught in the 1940 World Series for Detroit.

THE TIGER OUTFIELD, 1907 TO 1912. From left to right are Davy Jones, Ty Cobb, and Sam Crawford, the regular outfield throughout the pennant winning seasons. Jones came to the club at the end of the 1906 season from the Chicago Cubs and stayed through 1912. Crawford joined the club in 1903 and played through the 1917 season, batting over .300 eight times, with a high of .378 in 1911.

33

GEORGE MULLIN. "Wabash" George Mullin signed on with the Tigers over the winter of 1901–1902, the start of a distinguished 14-year career. Five times he won 20 games or more, winning 28 and losing 9 in 1909. George pitched and won both ends of a doubleheader on September 22, 1906. He would pitch the first no-hitter at Michigan and Trumbull on July 4, 1912, his 32nd birthday, against St. Louis.

WILLIAM DONOVAN. "Wild Bill" Donovan pitched for Washington in 1898 and Brooklyn in 1899, before coming to the Tigers in 1903. He gained his nickname from his pitching and aggressive base running. He had his best season in 1907, with a 25-4 record, and an American League high .862 winning percentage.

EDWARD SUMMERS. Coming to the Tigers in time for two of their three consecutive pennants, Ed won 24 and lost 12 with a 1.64 earned run average in 1908, and the next year went 19-9. He never regained his form after those two seasons. On September 25, 1908, he pitched and won both games of a doubleheader against the Athletics, with two complete games. Ed was the first pitcher in modern baseball to homer twice in one game in 1910, the only two dingers of his career.

DONIE BUSH. Considered by many to be the all-time Tiger shortstop, Bush came to the team in 1908 and stayed through 1921. A good lead-off man with not too much power, he was an excellent base runner, stealing 403 bases. His career batting average was .250. He later managed in both leagues.

OPENING DAY, 1907. Brass bands and speeches by city officials always marked opening day in Detroit. The parade started from the players' hotels, with both teams participating, and continued right into the ball yard. The ceremonial first pitch would be thrown by a dignitary and was always caught by old-timer Charlie Bennett.

BENNETT PARK, 1900s. Ty Cobb may have just stolen his way around the bases from the way this crowd is reacting in the grandstands. Hats were the fashion of the day, and nobody went outside without one. These fans paid the top price of $1.25 for a reserved seat in Frank Navin's ballpark.

FRANK NAVIN, 1900S. "Lucky Frank" Navin was trained as a lawyer and worked as an accountant for Sam Angus, the team's second owner. When the club was sold to William Yawkey in 1903, Navin bought $5,000 worth of stock and was made the club president, where he remained for 32 years.

HUGH JENNINGS. In his familiar "Ee-Yah" stance in the third base coaches' box, Hugh exhorts his team of Tigers on. He was captain and shortstop of the powerful Baltimore Orioles, National League champs for three straight years, 1894–96. He won three straight pennants with the Tigers in 1907–1909, but never a World Series or another flag, even though he remained through the 1920 season.

BENNETT PARK, 1908. The overflowing Saturday afternoon crowd watches Detroit play St. Louis on their way to another American League pennant. The Detroit Police Department is out in force to keep the crowd in line, who would sometimes take disagreements with umpires to an extreme. These are the "cranks" in right field, some of whom view the game from rather dangerous positions hanging from the fence.

BENNETT PARK, 1908. Colorful advertisements adorn the outfield fences, this time in the left field corner. In the lower right, outfielder Davy Jones poses for the camera, which also captures a good view of the "wildcat" stands outside the fence. These were illegal seats, and Frank Navin spent years attempting to have them permanently demolished.

DETROIT "TIGERS"~1908. AMERICAN LEAGUE CHAMPIONS

AMERICAN LEAGUE CHAMPIONS, 1908. For the second year in a row, the Tigers captured the American League pennant, winning 90 and losing 63 games for a .588 average. They finished only 1/2 game ahead of the Cleveland Indians, the issue being decided on the last game of the season with a 7-0 victory over Chicago. The Tigers batted .264 as a team and had a 2.40 ERA.

THE 1909 DETROIT TIGERS. The two-time defending American League Champions were aiming at an unprecedented third title and exploded to a fast start, holding first place for all but one day from April 26 through August. At one point they won 14 games in a row, in a season where Ty Cobb captured the only Triple Crown in team history and George Mullin led the majors with a 29-8 record.

BENNETT PARK, 1908. Donie Bush is at bat in this late season game against the New York Yankees. Catcher Mike "Doc" Powers takes what might be a pitch-out that he called for. Mike died tragically in 1909 from internal injuries sustained while chasing a foul ball. Umpire Tim Hurst looks on.

AMERICAN LEAGUE CHAMPIONS, 1909. Frank Navin wondered if his team would ever be crowned World Champions as his Tigers were again defeated, this time by the Pittsburgh Pirates. Led by Honus Wagner, who batted .333 against Cobb's .231, the Nationals won the Series four games to three. American League president Ban Johnson laid all of the blame on that "damn National Leaguer Jennings."

BENNETT PARK, 1909. In late August, Connie Mack brought his Philadelphia Athletics into town, trying to catch Detroit. Here Ty Cobb slides hard into third base, spiking Frank Baker on the arm. The Athletics claimed that it was intentional and a lifetime suspension was considered for Cobb until Bill Kuenzel presented this photograph, which proved otherwise. The photo clearly shows Cobb's fade-away slide—away from Baker, who is out of the base path.

SAM CRAWFORD. "Wahoo Sam" Crawford came out of Wahoo, Nebraska, and started his major league career with Cincinnati in 1899. He came to the Tigers in 1903 and stayed through the 1917 season. He had eight seasons in which he batted over .300 for the Tigers, his best in 1911 with a .371 average. Sam patrolled the outfield with Cobb and Jones and has the most triples in a lifetime at 312.

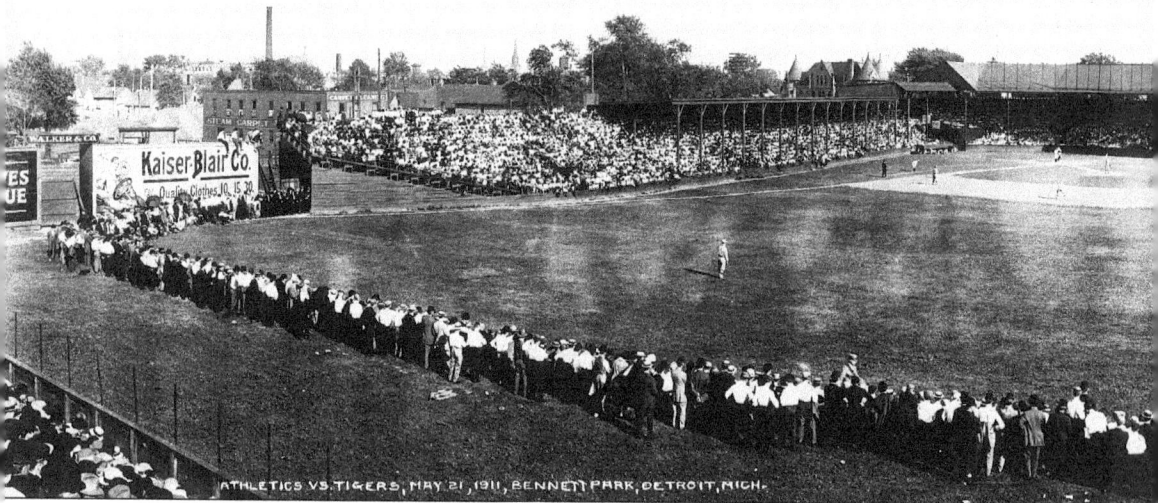

ATHLETICS AND TIGERS, 1911. A covered grandstand and bleacher seats have been added to Bennett Park, increasing seating capacity to 14,000 people. There is still an overflow crowd on May 21, 1911, to watch the hottest team in the American League. The Tigers enjoyed a .408 edge over the rest of the competition, prompting the newspaper

to crow, "The Tigers can't lose and the rest of them might as well quit the race." The team stayed in first for all but one day through August 4—they completely unraveled and struggled in the stretch to stagger home a poor second, 13 1/2 games behind Connie Mack's Philadelphia Athletics.

OPPOSITE PAGE: BENNETT PARK FROM THE GRANDSTANDS, 1911. Here is an exciting shot of Bennett Park action from the grandstand, behind home plate. It was a game that was played on May 12, 1911, between the Tigers and the New York Yankees. It is the bottom of the seventh and Sam Crawford digs in against New York's Ray Caldwell. The crowd is still buzzing from when, moments earlier, Ty Cobb stole home on Caldwell and catcher Ed Sweeney, the record holder for stolen bases by a Yankee catcher (19 bases in 1914). The team was on a roll, winning 21 out of their first 23 games, and was well out in front by the middle of May.

NAVIN FIELD, 1912. Navin Field opened on April 20, 1912, two days late because of rain and wet grounds. Over the previous winter, the old wooden stands had been torn down and replaced with a new concrete-and-steel single-covered deck. The field has also been turned around, home plate being moved 90 degrees to the west, which is its

present location. This was done to give the hitter the advantage of batting with the sun. In the first inning of the first game played, Ty Cobb can be seen stealing home with that fade-away slide. Cleveland's Ted Easterly tries to tag him, to no avail. Rookie first baseman Del Gainor is the batter.

WILLIAM A. KUENZEL, 1911. Bill Kuenzel became one of the first full-time newspaper photographers in the country when, at age 17, he quit his job with a local engraving company to join the *Detroit News* in 1901. From then until 1952, he covered every Tiger opening day game. But baseball was not the only item to be caught in his camera. He photographed every 20th-century American President, except McKinley, through 1952, as well as countless sports, grand opera, stage, screen, political, and Arctic exploration celebrities. Kuenzel was the first photographer to take a baseball action picture and to fly and take pictures from the air. He died from cancer in 1964.

Three

THE 1920S

THE DETROIT TIGERS OF 1922. Pictured from left to right are as follows: (front row) Fothergill, Rigney, Dauss, Frank Navin, President, Cobb, Manager, Woodall, and Veach; (middle row) Blue, Cutshaw, Manion, Heilman, Jones, Johnson, Moore, Olsen, Haney, Duggan, and Trainer; (back row) Bassler, Oldham, Ehmke, Pillette, Cole, Halloway, Holling, Howley, Clark, and Flagstead. Looking more like businessmen than ballplayers, these Tigers of 1922 compiled their first winning season in three years and finished third with 79 wins and 75 losses. Six regulars hit over .300 for the second straight year, with Cobb at .401. On the mound, Howard Emke kept batters ducking and still hit a club record 23 opponents. The decade saw mediocre teams, with the firing of Hughie Jennings as manager after 14 seasons and the hiring of Ty Cobb to replace him. In his first season at the helm, team batting jumped from seventh to first with a team record .316 and a league record of 1,724 hits.

NAVIN FIELD, 1920S. Looking north along Trumbull Avenue, this is a good view of the old ticket office and the right field fence. Soon due to receive a facelift with the addition of an upper deck on the grandstand, the ballpark was starting to assume its present facade. The seating capacity would increase to accommodate 23,000 fans.

THE NAVIN FIELD BOX OFFICE, 1920S. Fans line up to buy tickets for a home opener some time in the mid-1920s. In 1923, 900,000 of them would go through the turnstiles for the first time in team history. The following season, attendance would reach the million mark, making the Tigers the second big-league team to reach that milestone.

LUZERNE BLUE. Lu Blue was one of the finest fielding first basemen of all time. He came to the Tigers in 1921 and was the regular first baseman through the 1927 season. In his first season, he made 16 errors in 152 games for a .990 fielding average.

LU BLUE. Not only a smooth fielder, Lu would bat .309 in his first season with 33 doubles and a slugging average of .427. He would hit over .300 in four of his seven seasons as a Tiger, before being traded to the St. Louis Browns in 1928. Lu had a .287 lifetime batting average.

THE 1923 TIGER OUTFIELD. Pictured from left to right are Ty Cobb, Harry Heilman, Robert Veach, Robert Fothergill, and Heinie Manush. A second place finish for the 1923 Tigers was Cobb's highest finish as manager. This outfield would pound out over 650 hits, with Veach and Fothergill as part-timers. They would still finish 16 games behind the soon-to-be World Champion New York Yankees.

ROBERT VEACH. One of the all-time great Tiger outfielders, Bobby joined the Tigers in 1912 and played regularly until 1924, when he was traded to the Boston Red Sox. His best season was 1919, when he hit a league-high 45 triples and batted .355. He hit .321 in a pinch-hitting role in 1923.

ROBERT FOTHERGILL. Bob "Fat" Fothergill was one of the most popular players to wear a Tiger uniform. Nicknamed "Rotund Robert" because of his excessive weight, he joined the club in 1922 and stayed until the middle of the 1930 season. He was one of the greatest pinch-hitters of all time, compiling a .327 batting average in his nine years as a Tiger.

HARRY HEILMAN. Another one of the greatest hitters of all time, Heilman joined the Tigers in 1914 and played 17 seasons in the majors. He was a .342 lifetime hitter, leading the league in 1921, 1923, 1925, and 1927. He hit .394 in 1921, .403 in 1923, and .393 and .398 in 1925 and 1927 respectively. From 1934 to 1951, Heilman was the radio voice of the Tigers.

HEINIE MANUSH. Heinie replaced Ty Cobb as the center fielder for the Tigers. He was with Detroit from 1923 through 1927, when he was traded, along with Lu Blue, to St. Louis in one of the worst deals of all time. Manush led the league in batting in 1926 with a .378 average. In 1928, he missed the batting crown by one point and finished as a .330 lifetime slugger.

THE VETERAN AND THE ROOKIE, 1920S. Two of baseball's immortals converse at the ball park sometime during the mid-1920s. Ty Cobb is enjoying his last season as the Tiger manager, while Babe Ruth is gaining ascendancy as the Sultan of Swat. One era ends, another begins—the dead ball era of Cobb and the home run era of Ruth.

EDWIN WELLS. Ed was one of the slowest working pitchers in the American League when he pitched for the Tigers from 1923 through 1927. In his best season, 1926, he won 12 and lost 10. Although a career losing pitcher, as a rookie he struck out Babe Ruth with two on base the first time he faced him.

ULYSSES SIMPSON GRANT STONER. "Lil" Stoner was another mediocre pitcher, joining the Tigers in 1922 and staying through 1929, when he was traded to the Philadelphia Phillies. Stoner served up what is thought to be the longest home run ever hit by Babe Ruth. It went over the old right field bleachers, down a side street, and kept going.

JOHNNY BASSLER. Johnny came to the Tigers in 1921 after two earlier seasons with the Cleveland Blues, or Naps, as they were called then. He was the Tigers' regular catcher for seven seasons, and is considered by some to be the best catcher in the league at that time. He had an ability to out-guess opponents and had splendid judgment. His best season batting was in 1924, when he hit .346.

TIGER MANAGEMENT PLOTS STRATEGY, 1929. Roger Bresnahan (on the left) and Bucky Harris discuss Bengal strategy during the 1929 campaign. Bresnahan spent only a few seasons as a coach with Detroit, but his major league career dates back to 1897, and his debut as a pitcher. He later became the New York Giants first-string catcher, backstopping the great Christy Mathewson.

ONE THAT GOT AWAY. Bucky Harris chats with Washington's Walter Johnson, some time during the 1929 season. Harris was the player-manager for the Nationals and led them to two American League pennants. He took over for George Moriarty for several seasons. Walter Johnson, the greatest right-handed pitcher in American League history, was once a Tiger farm team property.

OWEN CARROLL AND HASKELL BILLINGS. These were two Tiger pitchers who never quite lived up to their promise. Carroll came out of Holy Cross University in Massachusetts, where he won 49 and lost 1 in four years. He came to the team in 1925 and stayed until 1930. His best season was in 1928 when he went 16-12. "Josh" Billings was one of the first pitchers to wear glasses. In three seasons he won 10 and lost 15.

JOHN HENRY NEUN. Johnny Neun was with the Tigers as a part-time first baseman from 1925 through 1928. He is perhaps best remembered for an unassisted triple play that he made on May 31, 1927, against the Indians. He had another great day on July 9, 1926, when he went five-for-five and also stole five bases.

ELON C. HOGSETT. Elon was a full-blooded Native American and, as could be expected of the time, was nicknamed "Chief." He came up to the Tigers in 1929 and remained through the 1937 season. This hard-throwing left-hander was also good with a bat, enjoying a .293 average in 1930 and a .226 lifetime average.

CLYDE MANION, 1922. "Pete" Manion was a light-hitting catcher whose defensive skills and ability to handle pitchers kept him in the major leagues for 14 years as a backup. He had a lifetime batting average of .217, but his fielding averages never went below .850. In 1928 he went to the St. Louis Browns.

JOHN KERR. John was a native of San Francisco and a favorite in the Pacific Coast League when he came over to the Tigers in 1923 as a second baseman and shortstop. His career batting average is .266, and when he went to the Senators in 1932 he was the roommate and constant companion of the enigmatic Moe Berg.

CHARLIE GEHRINGER. Former Tiger star Bobby Veach recommended that the team sign Charlie, and after one year at the University of Michigan they did. Two years later, in 1926, he became the regular second baseman. One of baseball's most sure-handed infielders, he was taciturn and undemonstrable, earning the nickname "The Mechanical Man." Teammate Doc Cramer once said "You wind him up on Opening Day and forget him."

FRANK O'ROURKE. "Blackie," a dark-complected native of Ontario, Canada, spent more than 70 years in major league baseball. His career began in 1912, and he played with four teams before arriving in Detroit as the second baseman in 1925. He came down with the measles in 1926, and rookie Charlie Gehringer took his place. He finished his career as a scout for the Yankees in 1983.

Dale Alexander. "Moose" was a rookie first baseman in 1929 who batted .343 and belted out 25 home runs in his first year. He also committed 18 errors with an iron glove that would prove to be his downfall. By 1931 his fielding had improved, but his home run swing disappeared and he was traded to the Boston Red Sox.

Replacement Managers, 1927. Ty Cobb and George Moriarty shake hands during the 1927 or 1929 season. Cobb finished his career playing for Connie Mack's Athletics in 1928, and Moriarty survived two seasons as the Tigers skipper before returning to the umpire's ranks for 11 years.

Detroit Stars, 1921

THE DETROIT STARS, 1921. Charter members of the Negro National League in 1920 were the Detroit Stars, who played their home games at Mack Park, on Mack and Fairview Avenues, on the city's east side. They played ball on Sundays and would pack the park with crowds just as enthusiastic and knowledgeable as those found across town. Among the Stars' shining players were Ted "Double Duty" Radcliffe, Pete Hill, Bill Gatewood, Norman "Turkey" Stearnes, and Bruce Petway, a catcher who threw out Ty Cobb while attempting to steal in an exhibition game in Cuba in 1910. The Stars proved to be one of the League's more stable teams, existing 13 consecutive seasons from 1919 to 1931.

Four

THE 1930s

THE DETROIT TIGERS, WORLD CHAMPIONS OF 1935. Pictured from left to right are as follows: (front row) Pete Fox, Jo-Jo White, Coach Cy Perkins, Manager Mickey Cochrane, Coach Del Baker, Flea Clifton, and Goose Goslin; (second row) Charley Gehringer, Hugh Shelley, Marvin Owen, Ray Mayworth, Schoolboy Rowe, Elden Auker, and Hank Greenberg; (third row) Heinie Schuble, Vic Sorrell, Frank Reiber, Joe Sullivan, Alvin Crowder, and Gerald Walker; (back row) Trainer Denny Carroll, Bill Rogell, Elon Hogsett, Mascot Joe Roggin, and Tommy Bridges. For the first time since 1900, the Tigers have finally captured the World Championship crown, defeating the Chicago Cubs four games to two. The Tigers won the American League pennant with a 93-58 record and a .616 winning percentage.

NAVIN FILED, 1930. Opening day ceremonies take place before a capacity crowd as the American flag is about to be raised in center field. An upper deck was added to the grandstand prior to the 1923 season, increasing the seating capacity to 23,000 fans. During the Depression, attendance at home games fell from 11,000 to 4,000 per game.

FRANK NAVIN AND BUCKY HARRIS, 1930s. Both the owner and the manager look pensive as they watch the team warm up during the early 1930s. Navin had yet to see his Bengals win a title, and perhaps he is thinking it might be time to change skippers. Harris had led the Senators to a couple of pennants, but had no such luck in Detroit. He was fired in 1933.

GORDON STANLEY COCHRANE, 1934. "Mickey" was one of the all-time great catchers, starting out with the Philadelphia Athletics in 1925. At the end of the 1933 season, he was sold to the Tigers for $100,000 and a catcher by the name of John Pasek. He was given the manager's job for the 1934 season and surprised the baseball world by winning the American League pennant for the first time in 25 years.

ELDON AUKER. "Big Six" came to the Tigers in 1933 and pitched in the first major league game he ever saw. He had a wicked submarine delivery and went 3-3 in his rookie year. His best season was 1935, when he won 18 and lost 7 with the American League's best winning percentage of .720. He was traded to the Boston Red Sox in 1938.

HANK GREENBERG. "Hammerin' Hank" signed with Detroit in 1930 and served some time in the minors until called up to the big club in 1933. He was 6 feet, 4 inches tall, weighed 215 pounds, and turned into one of the most fearsome sluggers in baseball history. In his rookie year he hit 33 doubles, 12 home runs, and had a .301 batting average.

CHARLIE GEHRINGER. In explaining the quiet nature of "The Mechanical Man," Mickey Cochrane said, "Charlie says 'hello' on opening day, 'good-bye' on closing day, and in between hits .350." Charlie had more than two hundred hits in seven different seasons in his career and was a polished fielder with quick hands. He rarely lost a ball he got his glove on.

TOMMY BRIDGES. A graduate of the University of Tennessee, Tommy was expected to follow in his father's footsteps and become a country doctor. He chose baseball instead and started for the Tigers in 1930. He had a blazing fastball, but his wicked curve baffled major league batters for over a decade. In 1932, Tommy lost a bid for a perfect game against Washington. With two out in the ninth, pinch-hitter Dave Harris singled. The Tigers won 13-0.

LYNWOOD ROWE. "Schoolboy" Rowe came up from Arkansas to help pitch the Tigers to three pennants and was one of the top American League right-handers of the Depression era. He came up in 1933 and had a 24-8 record during the 1934 season. Sixteen of his wins were consecutive, tying the American League record. He was often used as a pinch-hitter and had a lifetime average of .263.

BILLY ROGELL. Billy joined the Tigers in 1930 after a stint with the Boston Red Sox. He was a key factor in the team's two pennant wins, being the shortstop in the keystone combination with Charlie Gehringer. He was a switch hitter, good in the clutch, and led American League shortstops in fielding for three years, 1935–37.

MARVIN OWEN. Marv Owen came up to the Tigers in 1933 and anchored third base for five years. He was a dangerous clutch hitter, and in 1934 he batted .317 and knocked in 96 runs. His four infield teammates each knocked in over one hundred runs that season. During the 1934 World Series, he was involved in a scrap at third base when the Cardinals' Ducky Medwick slid in unnecessarily hard.

ERVIN FOX. "Pete" Fox was one of the American League's better offensive and defensive outfielders and a mainstay for the Tigers during the 1930s. He was also a good doubles hitter and could occasionally hit home runs. He batted over .300 each season from 1935 through 1937, and was the top batter in the 1935 World Series, getting ten hits for a .385 batting average.

BARNEY McCOSKY. Barney hit .300 in six of his first seven seasons for the Tigers, starting in 1939. He was the league's best lead-off hitter in his first two seasons, batting .311 and .340 respectively. He was a better-than-average outfielder, leading the league in putouts with 428 during the 1939 season.

LEON ALLEN GOSLIN. Nicknamed "Goose" because of his large nose, Goslin came to Detroit after successful seasons with the Senators and Browns. One of the famous "G-Men" (with Gehringer and Greenberg), Goose hit .305 in 1934 while playing left field for the Tigers, with a .953 fielding percentage. He drove in the winning run in game six of the 1935 World Series.

GERALD AND HARVEY WALKER. "Gee" and "Hub" Walker came to the Tigers as rookie outfielders in 1931. Hub (left) was sent down to the minors for more conditioning but would return for good in 1935, while his younger brother became one of the more popular Tigers, even though he had a bad habit of not paying attention while on the base paths.

AMERICAN LEAGUE CHAMPIONS, 1934. The J.L. Hudson Company unfurled this huge banner before the start of the World Series against the St. Louis Cardinals. It was Detroit's first pennant since 1909, and the city celebrated. The team turned in a 101-victory season, taking over first place on August 1 and finishing seven games ahead of the second-place New York Yankees. They hit for a team average of .300, with Gehringer leading the way at .356. Mickey Cochrane was voted the league's Most Valuable Player, hitting .320 with 76 RBIs and a .988 fielding average, in a year when Lou Gehrig won the Triple Crown.

NAVIN FIELD, 1934. Navin Field is decorated with red, white, and blue bunting, and the crowd settles in to watch the Tigers battle the St. Louis Cardinals in the World Series. The two teams would split the first two games in Detroit, then the Tigers took two out of three in St. Louis, only to drop the next two. Frank Navin spent the winter brokenhearted.

BABE RUTH PAYS A VISIT TO DETROIT. The Sultan of Swat pays a visit to the Detroit dugout to wish the two teams good luck. From left to right are "Dizzy" Dean, Frankie Frisch, Babe Ruth, Mickey Cochrane, and "Schoolboy" Rowe. Dizzy's brother Paul would go the distance in game six to keep the Cardinals' chances alive.

A Conference in the Dugout, 1935. Mickey Cochrane and Charlie Gehringer discuss the horsehide during the 1935 season. They would smack the ball around for a .330 and .319 batting average, respectively, and the Tigers would repeat as American League champs. The team drew one million fans for the second time in team history, and they watched Hank Greenberg win his first of two League MVPs.

Charlie Wins a Car. Charley Gehringer and an unidentified automobile dealer stand beside a brand new car presented to him on the field. What more could "the mechanical man" ask for? Charley led the league in fielding assists at second base with 489, and in fielding average with .985, committing only 13 errors all year.

ACTION AT NAVIN FIELD. The infield is pulled way in as the Tigers are trying to bring the man home from third in this action shot. It seems that everybody in the yard is wearing a hat—mostly fedoras. Note the group of photographers positioned about 10 feet away from home plate.

BLEACHER CREATURES AT THE WORLD SERIES, 1935. These Detroiters are having the time of their lives watching their Tigers demolish the Chicago Cubs in World Series play. It is cold in early October, and the red hots are quite welcome. There is surely no mistaking the hot dog vendor dressed in white with that marvelous hat.

VIPs at the World Series, 1935. This scene from the box seats shows a disgruntled baseball commissioner and an unhappy owner. Judge Kenesaw Mountain Landis (right) looks as though he bet on the Cubs, while Colonel Jacob Ruppert still can't believe the Bengals passed his team for good back in July.

More Yankees in the House, 1935. The immortal Lou Gehrig stops to chat with Mickey Cochrane (left) and Marv Owen (right) during the 1935 World Series. Gehrig was in the prime of his career, having won baseball's Triple Crown in 1934, and was taking a rare post-season rest along with his team. He was soon to be stricken with the disease that bears his name.

WORLD SERIES ACTION, 1935. The crowd gets settled at the second game of the series. It is a sell-out crowd of over 46,000, with extra seats set up on the right-field, foul-line roof for out-of-town reporters. The Tigers had dropped the opener 3-0, and the crowd was pensive. The team responded with a four-run first inning, and Tommy Bridges went all the way in an 8-3 verdict.

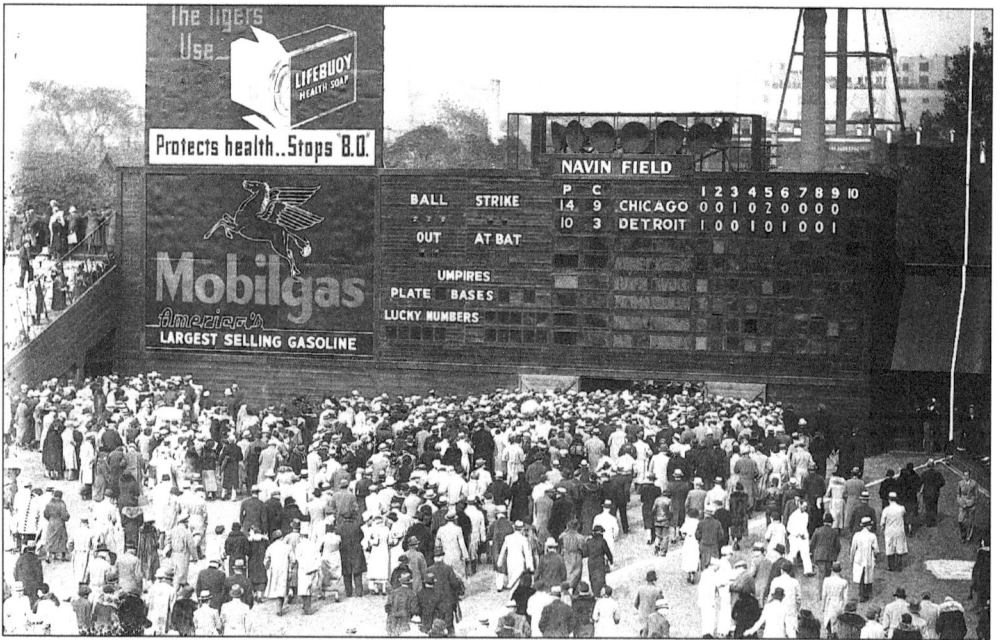

VICTORY AT LAST. The scoreboard reflects the final verdict as over 48,000 raucous fans file out of the park to celebrate the Tigers World Series victory. The contest was decided in the bottom of the ninth, when Cochrane scored from second on Goslin's single. He later said, "My greatest thrill in baseball was scoring that run."

NAVIN FIELD, 1936. A troop of Detroit's finest march out from home plate carrying the American League Champions banner for 1935 on opening day, 1936. Fan hopefuls waited to see if the Tigers could match their team record and win a third consecutive pennant. They were disappointed, as injuries to key players and disruptive influences led to a second-place finish.

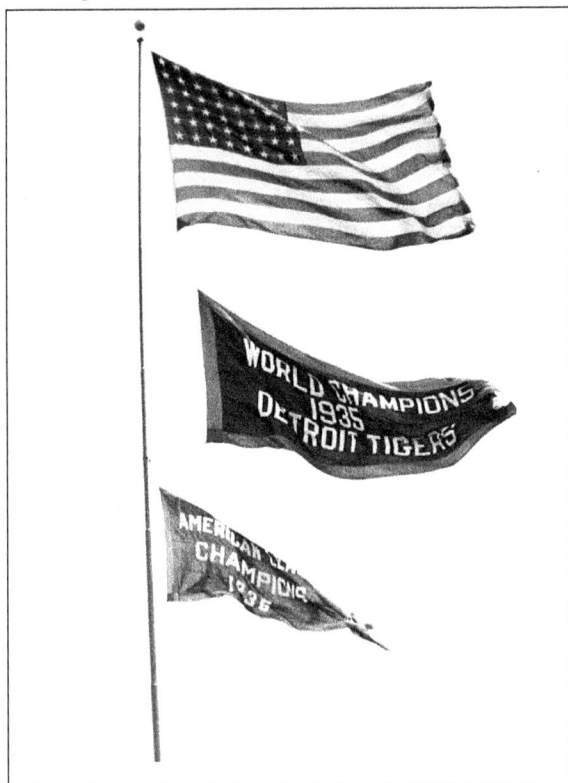

BANNERS FLY AT NAVIN FIELD, 1936. The second banner to be raised on opening day was the one everybody had hoped and prayed for: THE World Champions. After the sixth game victory, even poker-faced owner Frank Navin exclaimed over and over again, "I have waited 30 years for this day." It was a banner he would never see. In November 1935, he suffered a fatal heart attack.

Rudy York. Rudy York was always a threat at the plate at 6 feet, 1 inch, and 210 pounds, but couldn't break into the line up behind Hank Greenberg. Rudy, who was half Native American, finally got his chance in 1937 when, as a rookie, he broke Babe Ruth's record for home runs in one month with 18 in August. He also drove in 49 runs that month, another record.

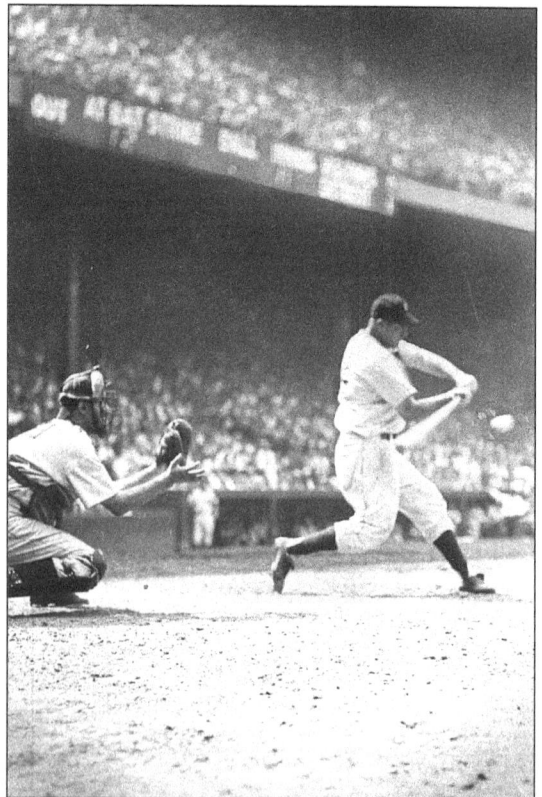

Hank Greenberg at Bat, 1939. "Hammerin" Hank connects on another one in this action scene during baseball's contrived centennial season, 1939. He would miss 17 games with an injury, as the team slipped into the second division. Charley Gehringer became the fourth Tiger to hit for the cycle on May 27, against the Browns, in perfect single-double-triple-home run succession.

Five

THE 1940S

THE DETROIT TIGERS, 1945. Pictured here, from left to right, are as follows: (front row) Cramer, Maier, Trout, Mills (coach), O'Neill (manager), Newhouser, Richards, and Mayo; (second row) Wilson, Mueller, Outlaw, Benton, McHale, Overmire, and Orrell; (third row) Webb, Borom, Pierce, Walker, Houtteman, Swift, York, and Cullenbine; (back row) Hoover, Hostetler, Welsh, Dr. Forsyth, and Trainer. The American League pennant winners finished this last World War II season with 88 wins and 65 losses, for a .575 winning percentage under Steve O'Neill. The Tigers had finished the first half of the decade with two pennants and a second-place finish. Quite a number of major league veterans were now armed forces veterans and were just now returning from active duty.

BRIGGS STADIUM, 1940s. This was the scene at the corner of Michigan and Trumbull since the late 1930s, when Walter O. Briggs added the finishing touches to give the ball park its present-day look. The team appears to have been present this day, as is evident from the foot traffic along Trumbull Avenue.

OPENING DAY LINEUP, 1940. Pictured here are, from left to right, McCosky, center field; Campbell, right field; Gehringer, second base; Greenberg, left filed; York, first base; Higgins, third base; Bartell, shortstop; Tebbetts, catcher; and Newsome, pitcher. Newcomers Bartell, Tebbetts, and Newsome would play crucial roles in the drive down the stretch to the American League flag.

WALTER O. BRIGGS SR. This fan, who owned a ball club, was so vocal that he was nearly ejected from the ballpark in 1902 by umpire Tom Connolly. He made his fortune in the auto body industry and became Frank Navin's silent partner in 1920. When Navin died in 1935, Briggs purchased the remaining stock in the club to become sole owner. He would reinvest the profits and add his own money to improve the club and the ballpark.

DEL BAKER. Del was a catcher during his 22-year playing career and was a Tiger coach until he replaced Mickey Cochrane as manager in 1938. He would manage the club through 1942 and, an expert sign-stealer, he would lead the Bengals to the 1940 pennant. They would eventually lose to the Cincinnati Reds.

LYNWOOD ROWE, 1940s.
"Schoolboy" Rowe had been with the Tigers since the 1933 season, but chronic arm trouble had forced him back to the minor leagues for conditioning. He came roaring back for the 1940 season, however, leading the American League in winning percentage with a 16-3 record. He was waived to the National League in 1942.

TOMMY BRIDGES, 1940s.
Another veteran Tiger pitcher was Tommy Bridges, a starter since the 1930 campaign. He had two World Series outings under his belt and would help pitch the Tigers to the 1940 flag with a 12-9 record. He would be called into the service in 1943 at the age of 37, but would return in time for the 1945 pennant run.

HENRY GREENBERG, 1940. A perennial all-star since his rookie season in 1930, Hank was quite the slugger, hitting 40 home runs in 1938, and giving chase to Babe Ruth's record the next season, finishing with 58 dingers. He tied Jimmy Foxx's record for right-handed hitters and set a record for most multi-home run games in a season with 11.

RUDY YORK AND HANK GREENBERG, 1940. In order to get the hard-hitting York's bat into the everyday line up, the Tigers asked Greenberg to shift to left field, a completely new position. Many credit Hank's willingness to do this as a key factor in the team's successful 1940 season. York hit 33 homers, but Greenberg earned his second MVP award with a .340 average, 41 home runs, and 150 runs batted in.

DICK BARTELL. "Rowdy Richard" is out at the plate, despite the collision, in this 1940 action scene. Bartell had been traded from the Chicago Cubs just in time for the pennant-winning season. An aggressive base runner, he would bat .233 for the year but turn in a .953 fielding average at shortstop.

WORLD SERIES PLAY, 1940. Charley Gehringer beats the throw to first baseman Mike McCormick to spoil a Cincinnati double play in the sixth inning of the second game on October 3. Barney McCosky is forced out at second, as umpire Lu Ballanfant positions himself to make the call. The Tigers won the game 7-2.

THE 1940 WORLD SERIES, GAME FIVE. Hank Greenberg connects for a three-run home run against Red's pitcher "Junior" Thompson, as the Bengals pounded out 13 hits and 8 runs to win going away. Bobo Newsome pitched a three-hit shutout in Detroit to put the Tigers up three games to two.

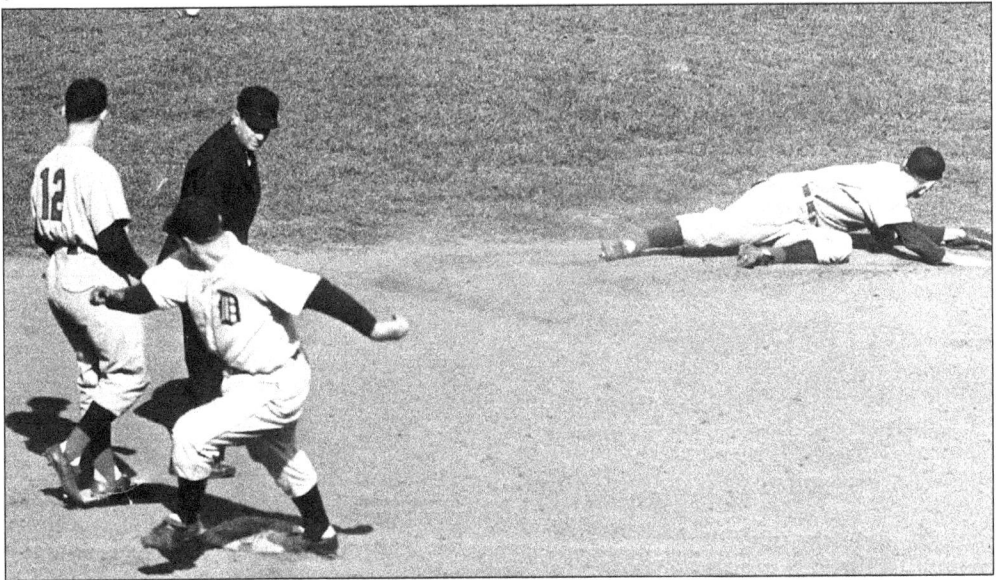

THROUGH THE MIDDLE. Here is more action from game five on October 6, 1940. Rudy York rounds second and takes off for third as the ball goes through the middle out to center field. The Tigers exploded for three runs in the third inning and four more in the fourth on their way to an 8-0 romp.

LOUIS NORMAN NEWSOME. "Bobo" Newsome came to the Tigers in 1939 in a trade with the St. Louis Browns. He had a 21-5 record in 1940 and was the hero of the World Series that year, winning two games and losing one in a great pitching duel. He showed great courage during the series—the day after he won the series opener 7-2, his father died suddenly of a heart attack.

GAME SEVEN, OCTOBER 9,1940. Billy Sullivan Jr., Tiger back-up catcher, scores the Bengals only run in the third inning on a throwing error. A great pitching duel between Newsome and the Reds' Paul Derringer saw the Tigers lose as the result of a two-run seventh inning. Newsome finished the series with a 1.38 earned run average.

CAMP CUSTER, MICHIGAN, 1941. Hank Greenberg poses on the steps of the barracks as he prepares to leave for active duty in the Pacific. Major League ball players were not exempt from the draft, although President Roosevelt had given the okay to continue to play the schedule during the war. Many players who would never have broken into the "bigs" got their chance.

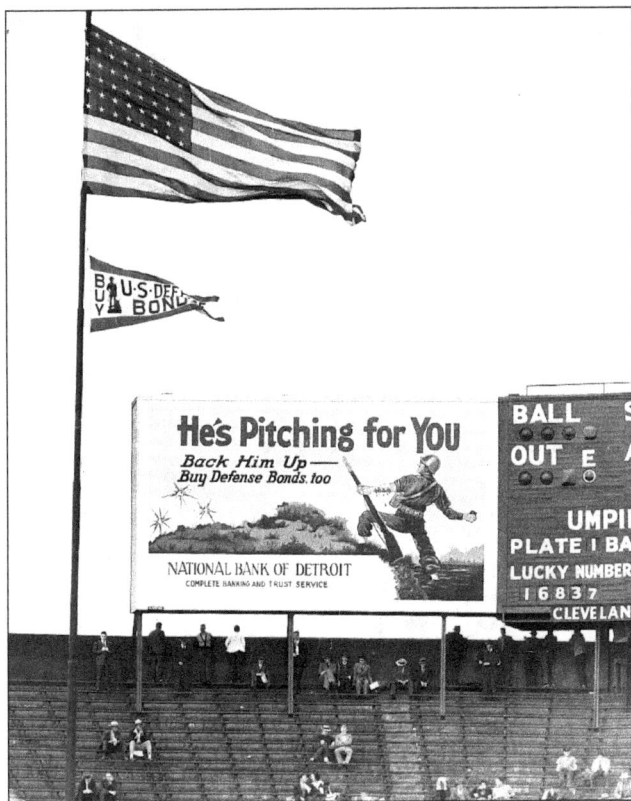

WARTIME BASEBALL, 1941– 1945. As the country geared up to defeat the Axis Powers, many reminders were given to the home front to support the war effort. The Briggs Stadium center field flag pole reminds fans to buy war bonds, and many advertisements managed to include baseball-type slogans in their attempts to drum up support for the boys at the front.

A Hero's Welcome, 1945. Steve O'Neill shakes the hand of returning veteran Hank Greenberg to welcome him back to the major league ranks. Other teammates greet him, as well as Rudy York (seated left), who looks on, all smiles. Greenberg would bat .311 in what remained of the season.

A Calm Discussion at Home, 1945. Umpire Hal Weafer gets some verbal instruction from Tiger catcher Bob Swift and manager Steve O'Neill on what the rule book says constitutes a balk. That is what Weafer called on Hal Newhouser (right), with the bases loaded in a game against the White Sox in the ninth inning. It gave Chicago a run and made the score 3-2, but Newhouser retired the next batter to save the win.

BRIGGS STADIUM, 1945. As World War II wound down, more and more Detroiters flocked back to the ball park to cheer their Tigers to another possible pennant. The team would respond, especially when the veterans returned to the line up, and just in time, too. The Tigers needed one victory in a season-ending double header in St. Louis.

PLAYING HARD TO WIN, AUGUST 1945. Right fielder Roy Cullenbine is out at third on Rudy York's hit in the sixth inning against the Philadelphia Athletics. George Kell makes the tag and, the next season, would report to the Tigers. Cullenbine, a native Detroiter, was an excellent outfielder with a terrific throwing arm.

RICHARD WAKEFIELD. Dick Wakefield was one of the first bonus babies to be signed by the Tigers off of the University of Michigan campus in 1941 for a then-record $52,000 and a new car. He played his first full season in 1943, hitting .316. He was in the service in 1944, but came back the next year and batted .355, nearly winning the pennant by himself.

VIRGIL TRUCKS, 1945. "Fire" Trucks was a right-handed control pitcher who started with the Tigers in 1941 but then entered military service and did not return until the end of the 1945 season. He still pitched the second game of the 1945 World Series less than a week after his discharge from the United States Navy, scattering seven hits on the way to a 4-1 victory.

HAROLD NEWHOUSER. "Prince Hal" was the most dominant pitcher in baseball for three years in the mid-1940s. He is the only pitcher to win consecutive MVP awards, doing so in 1944 and 1945. He signed with the Tigers while still in high school and appeared briefly at age 18 in 1939. He was up to stay in 1941.

PAUL HOWARD TROUT. "Dizzy" Trout was a colorful, fun-loving right hander who was a work horse for the Tigers in 1945, pitching six games and winning four over a nine-game, late season stretch. In game four of the World Series, he beat the Cubs 4-1 in a five-hitter.

WORLD SERIES ACTION, 1945. Pitcher Hal Newhouser fields "Peanuts" Lowrey's sacrifice bunt as Tiger fans watch in horror. Twenty-five-game winner Newhouser was shelled for seven runs in three innings, as the Cubs took the opener 9-0. Hank Borowy, a mid-year acquisition from the Yankees, threw a six-hit shutout to beat Detroit.

GAME SIX, OCTOBER 8, 1945. Hank Greenberg is congratulated by Roy Cullenbine and the Tiger batboy after his eighth-inning home run that tied the score at seven runs apiece. In the 12th inning, a drive hit by Cub third baseman Stan Hack got by Hank in left field, scoring pinch runner Bill Schuster for an 8-7 Cub victory.

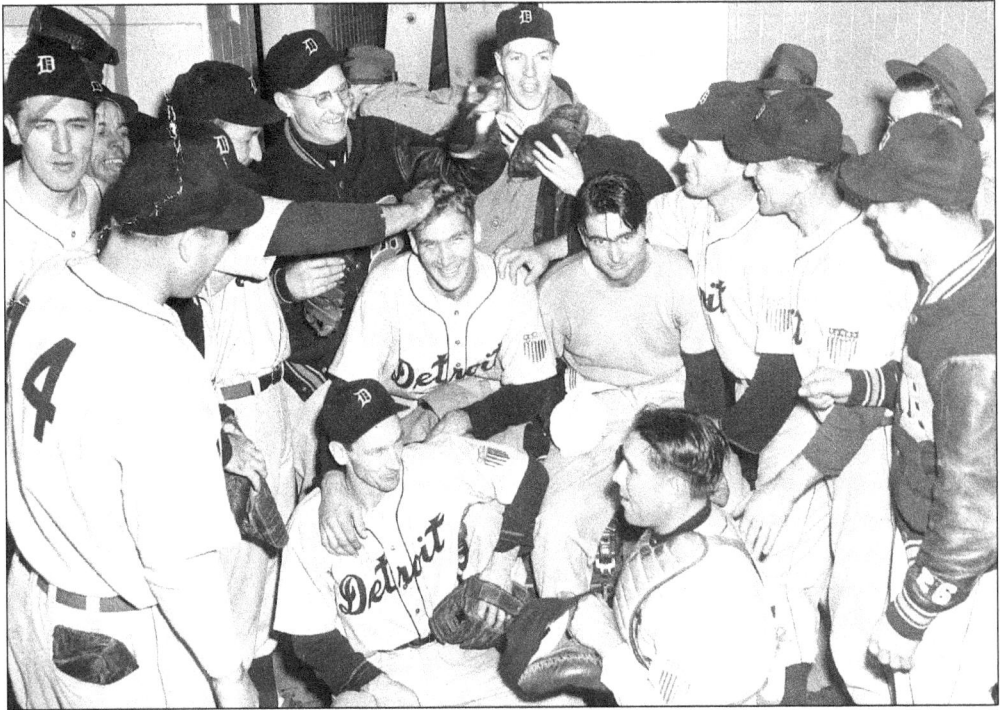

A WORLD SERIES CELEBRATION, 1945. The scene in the Tigers dressing room is one of jubilation, as the Bengals congratulate winning pitcher Hal Newhouser, who scattered ten hits and struck out ten Cubs to lead the club to its second World Championship. Hal set a World Series record with 22 strikeouts in his three appearances.

RETURNING VETERANS, 1946. These Tigers have just been released from service and have returned to the team. Pictured from left to right are as follows: (front row) Moore, White, Wertz, Mueller, Stone, Tebbetts, Hutchinson, Herson, and Riebe; (middle row) Blackwell, Tabacheek, Everson, Mullins, and Hitchcock; (back row) Erautt, Lake, Kerns, Horton, Wakefield, Lipon, Howerton, Scott, Moran, and Clark.

VIC WERTZ. Vic came to the Tigers for the start of the 1947 season as a powerful left-hand-hitting outfielder. He hit .288 in a part-time role before becoming a regular in 1948. In 1949, he drove in 133 runs and 123 followed in 1950. His was the long drive that made Willy Mays famous in 1954.

THE 1948 DETROIT TIGERS STARTING LINE UP. Pictured right to left are O'Neill, manager; Berry, shortstop; Mayo, second base; Evers, center field; Wakefield, left field; Wertz, right field; Kell, third base; Vico, first base; Swift, catcher; and Newhouser, pitcher. After finishing second two seasons in a row, the Tigers took a dive to fifth in a season known for bad trades. Native Detroit pitcher Billy Pierce, considered expendable, was dealt to Chicago, where he won 200 games over 18 seasons.

Six

THE 1950s

THE 1951 DETROIT TIGERS. Pictured from left to right are as follows: (front row) Bob Mavis, Wayne McLeland, George Lerchen, Carl Linhart, Al Federoff, Harold Daugherty, and Hal White; (second row) Gerald Preddy, Coach Rick Ferrell, Coach Ted Lyons, Manager Red Rolfe, Coach Dick Bartell, Vic Wertz, and Virgil Trucks; (third row) Trainer Jack Homel, Charlie Keller, Neil Berry, Pat Mullin, Hank Borowy, Bob Swift, Harold Newhouser, Frank House, Marlin Stuart, and Earl Johnson; (fourth row) Paul Trout, Ray Herbert, Art McConnell, Ken Fremming, Ted Grey, Joe Ginsburg, John Groth, and Paul Calvert; (fifth row) Fred Hutchinson, John Lipon, George Kell, Walter Evers, Dick Kryhoski, Saul Rogovin, Steve Souchock, Aaron Robinson, and Don Kolloway. This Tiger team never rose above third place all year, finishing a dismal fifth.

THE STARTING LINE-UP, 1951. The starting line-up on opening day saw Lipon, shortstop; Berry, third base; Kolloway, first base; Wertz, right field; Evers, left field; Groth, center field; Priddy, second base; Ginsburg, catcher; and Newhouser, pitcher. Only one Tiger hit above .300, and he was not even in the line-up in April. George Kell finished third in the league at .319.

FIRST-STRING TIGER PITCHERS. Pictured are, from left to right are, as follows: (front) Virgil Trucks, Art Houtteman, Frank Overmire, and Fred Hutchinson; (back) Dizzy Trout and Hal Newhouser. A mixture of rookies and veterans, the pitching staff only managed a 4.25 earned run average. There was only one American League team to have never finished last—until 1952. The Tigers won only 50 games (still a team record), while losing 104 to finish eighth.

94

GEORGE KELL. George came to the Tigers in a trade with the Athletics for Barney McCoskey in 1946. He continued to play third base in Detroit until the middle of 1952. He was the one bright spot in 1951, batting .319, leading the league in hits. He was also tied for second in doubles.

ACTION AT THE CORNER, 1950S. Kell slides safely into third. In 1949 he won his only batting title, depriving Ted Williams of his third Triple Crown. Kell batted .300 in eight consecutive seasons, starting in 1946. He was one of the premier third basemen in the game, leading American League third basemen seven times in fielding and four times in assists.

BRIGGS STADIUM, 1951. The new Tiger ticket office is dressed up to celebrate Detroit's 250th birthday on July 24, 1951, with patriotic bunting and the official logo of the celebration. In the midst of all the partying, the selective service was gearing up for the Korean War. Tiger pitchers Art Houtteman and his replacement Ray Herbert were both drafted.

THE ALL-STAR GAME, 1951. Detroit hosted its second All-Star Game (the first was in 1941) on July 10, 1951. Here George Kell is greeted by none other than Ted Williams of the Boston Red Sox after Kell's solo home run. Over 52,000 watched the game as the National League beat the junior circuit 8-3.

96

ALBERT KALINE. "Mr. Tiger" was signed by Detroit right off the Baltimore sandlots and never played one inning in the minor leagues. Al played right field in his first game on June 25, 1953, at the ripe old age of 17. He made playing right field into an art form, winning ten Gold Gloves in eleven years.

HARVEY KUENN. This Tiger bonus baby reached the majors after just 63 games in the minors in his first professional season. Kuenn won the 1953 Rookie of the Year Award, batting .308 with a league-leading 209 hits, setting a Major League rookie record with 679 at-bats and an American League rookie record with 167 singles.

BONUS BABIES, 1954. These three Tiger cubs represent an investment of $120,000. Reno Bertoria (left) got a $25,000 signing bonus, Bob Miller (center) $60,000, and Al Kaline $35,000. Bertoria had speed and good hands, Miller debuted as a 17-year-old left hander, and Kaline became a permanent fixture in right field for 22 seasons.

A THRILL FOR THE ROOKIES, 1950s. A Tiger legend of the past shakes hands with two future Tiger stars. Ty Cobb put one arm around Harvey Kuenn while grasping the paw of Al Kaline. In 1955, Kaline would become the youngest American League batting champion ever, shading out Ty Cobb for the honor by a couple of months.

THE 1955 TIGER SPRING TRAINING SQUAD. With a few exceptions, this is the team that started out the 1955 season with high hopes. It was not to be, although there were some shining moments. Al Kaline won the batting crown, Harvey Kuenn hit .308, and Ray Boone tied for the league lead for RBIs with 116. Billy Hoeft led Tiger pitchers with a 16-7 record as the team finished fifth again.

SPRING TRAINING, 1956. Pictured from left to right are Al Kaline, Bill Tuttle, Ray Boone, Steve Gromek, Spike Briggs, Ned Garver, Frank House, and Virgil Trucks. These Tigers take a break to pose with Tiger president Walter O. "Spike" Briggs Jr., who took over the reins after his father's death in 1952. The Tigers would finish fifth again, but would lead the league in hitting.

JIM BUNNING. This tall, lanky right hander came to the Tigers in 1955 and remained with the team through the 1963 season, when he was traded to the Philadelphia Phillies. He was the first pitcher to win over 100 games or record over 1,000 strikeouts in each league. He threw a no-hitter on July 20, 1958, for Detroit, and a perfect game for the Phillies on June 21, 1964.

FRANK LARY. The "Yankee Killer" debuted for the Tigers in 1954, and by 1956 the fireballer emerged as the ace of a strong Tiger staff. He led the American League with 21 wins that season. He was always tough on the New York Yankees, sporting a 5-1 record against them in 1956 and a 7-0 record against them in 1958—the first time since 1916 that the Yankees were beaten seven times in one season by one pitcher.

100

PAUL FOYTACK. Paul was up briefly with the Tigers in 1953 and back to stay in 1955. Early on he had control problems, but ultimately became a solid member of the pitching staff, twice winning 15 and twice 14 games from 1956 to 1959. He was traded to the Los Angeles Angels in mid-season, 1963.

HAPPY TIGER TRIO. Winning pitcher Paul Foytack happily hugs his hitting hero teammates Red Wilson (left) and Eddie Yost (right) after the Tigers defeated the New York Yankees 4-0 at Yankee Stadium on August 6, 1959. Foytack threw a three-hitter while Wilson and Yost each hit a home run.

ALFRED MANUEL MARTIN. "Billy" Martin was a fine Yankee second baseman until traded to the Kansas City Athletics in 1957. He was part of a 12-player trade with Detroit in November 1957. He played shortstop during his one season as a Tiger player in 1958. He batted an honest .255, with 7 home runs and 42 runs batted in.

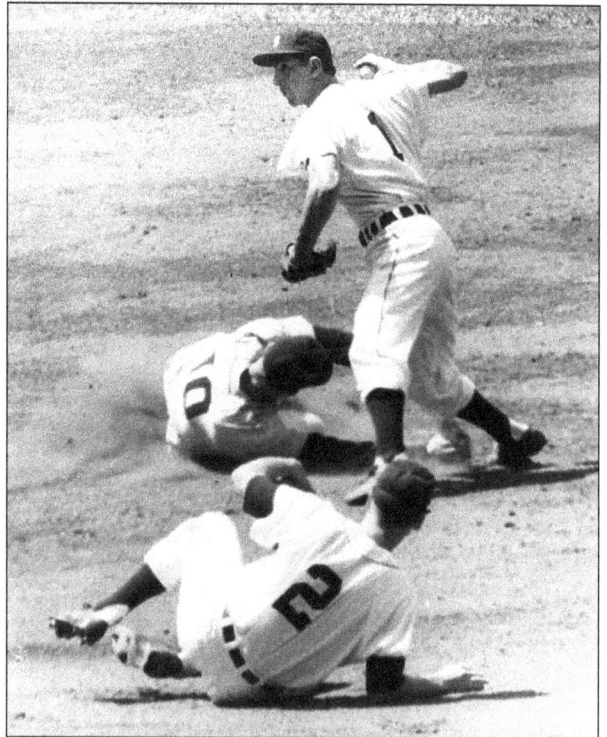

ACTION UP THE MIDDLE, 1958. Second baseman Frank Bolling (number ten) hits the dirt as he fields a grounder off the bat of Mickey Mantle, but not before tossing in time to Billy Martin to force a sliding Tony Kubek. Bolling led the league in assists with 445, fielding at a healthy .985 average.

THE TIGER HIT PARADE, 1950S. The Bengal line-up was loaded with sluggers like these all through the mid- to late 1950s. During one season Kaline, Charley Maxwell, and Ray Boone each hit 25 home runs and Kuenn, Kaline, and Boone each hit .300. Kuenn led the league in hits with 196. Kaline was second with 194 and second in RBIs with 128.

NO SHORTAGE OF SOUTHPAWS, 1950S. These Tigers pitchers are all left handers. From left to right, Billy Hoeft, Al Aber, Bob Miller, Bill Froats, Gene Host, and Jim Brady were all potential starters during the mid-1950s. All but Froats became regulars. Bill pitched in one game, a total of two innings in 1955, for his complete major league totals.

DON KOLLAWAY. Don was a first and second baseman, coming to the Tigers in a trade with the Chicago White Sox in 1949 for Earl Rapp. He stayed with the team as the regular first baseman and then a part-time player until 1953. He had a career batting average of .272.

BENGAL ACTION, 1958. A fierce slide by shortstop Billy Martin beats Cleveland's Minnie Minoso's throw to catcher Russ Nizon. Billy had singled and then scored from second base on Al Kaline's hit to left. The next batter, Ray Boone, gives coaching advice. The Tigers were victorious.

OSWALDO JOSE PICHARDO. Ozzie Virgil was the first Dominican to play in the major leagues and the first African American to play for the Detroit Tigers. He joined the team from the Giants in 1958 and went five for five in his first game with them, on his way to a .244 rookie season. Ozzie played third base part time behind Jim Bunning and helped him notch the team's fourth no-hitter with a .981 fielding average. He stayed with the Tigers until the middle of the 1960 season, when he was traded to Kansas City. He also had stops in Baltimore and Pittsburgh before beginning to coach for the San Francisco Giants in 1969.

CHARLIE LAU. Charley hailed from Romulus, Michigan, and started his career with the Tigers in 1956, where he was used sparingly as a catcher. He was a lifetime .180 hitter until 1962, when he radically changed his batting style and jumped his average up to .294. After his career, he became one of the most respected batting coaches of his time.

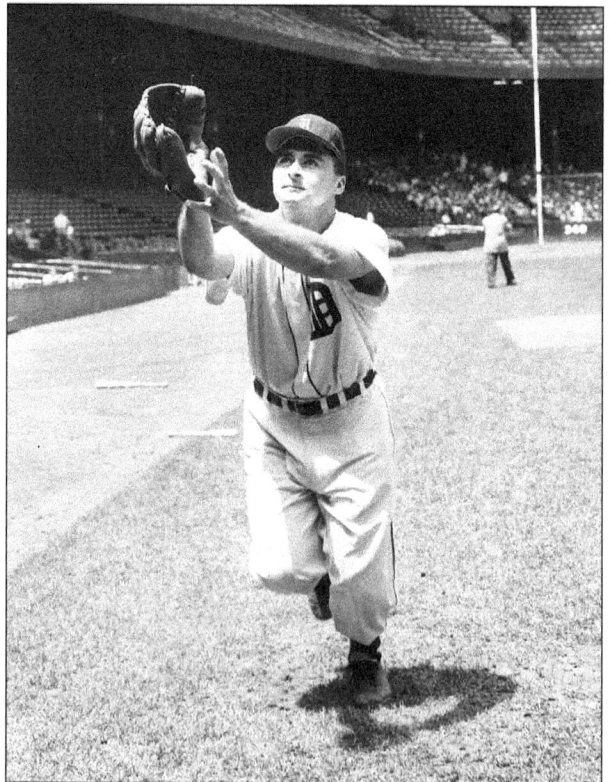

CHARLIE MAXWELL. "Sunday Punch" was raised in Paw Paw, Michigan, and came to Detroit via the Boston Red Sox and Baltimore Orioles in 1955. He was especially successful batting on Sundays, and for a five-year stretch (1956–60) hit well on most of the other days as well. In 1956 he set career highs in batting (.326) and slugging (.534) to go with 28 home runs.

A TYPICAL TIGER HOME OPENER, 1950s. Everybody is playing hooky to attend the opening day game, always started as an afternoon affair. Playing to nearly one million fans a season, the Tiger teams were supported through good times and bad. They are nothing if not the most vocal, best-dressed fans in the major leagues.

DON MOSSI. The "Sphinx" was acquired from Cleveland in a trade for Billy Martin and Al Cicotte in November 1958, as one of baseball's best bullpen aces. The Tigers made him a starter and he responded with a 17-9 record, 15 complete games, and a 3.36 earned run average.

JOHNNY GROTH. Johnny broke into the big leagues in 1949 after an all-star season with Buffalo in 1948 when he hit .340 and 30 home runs. In 1950 he hit .306 with 12 home runs and 85 RBIs. At one point he had eight consecutive hits. Johnny was never able to duplicate his 1950 totals, despite a ten-year career.

TIGER TRIO, 1950s. Pictured left to right are Al Kaline, Ray Boone, and Bucky Harris. Back for a second time managing was Bucky Harris, who first managed the Bengals from 1929 through 1933. The Tigers had a revolving door for managers during the decade, and Harris only survived for two seasons, 1955 and 1956.

Seven

THE 1960s

THE DETROIT TIGERS, 1968. Pictured from left to right areas follows: (front row) Don Wert, John Wyatt, Tony Cuccinello, Wally Moses, Mayo Smith, Hal Naragon, John Sain, Wayne Comer, Willie Horton, and Mickey Lolich; (second row) John Hand (equipment), Bill Behm (trainer), Julio Moreno (batting practice pitcher), Jim Northrup, Ray Oyler, Earl Wilson, Fred Lasher, Don McMahon, Al Kaline, and Charles C. Creedon (traveling secretary); (third row) Dick Tracewski, Norm Cash, Ed Mathews, Jim Price, Jon Warden, Denny McLain, Gates Brown, John Hiller, and Dick McAuliffe; (back row) Roy Face, Bob Christian, Mickey Stanley, Joe Sparma, Daryl Patterson, Pat Dobson, Tom Matchick, and Bill Freehan. These are the American League Champions as they make ready to face the defending champion St. Louis Cardinals in World Series competition. Detroit took first place for keeps on May 10 and breezed to the pennant by 12 games. They won 103 and lost 59 for a .636 winning percentage.

HANK AGUIRRE. Hank came to the Tigers as a left-handed reliever from the Cleveland Indians in February of 1958. In 1962 he was switched from the bullpen to the starting rotation and answered the call by leading the league in earned run average with a 2.21 mark. A native Californian, he was a notoriously poor hitter, posting an .085 lifetime mark.

THE VOICE OF THE TIGERS, 1961. Ernie Harwell began broadcasting major league baseball for the Brooklyn Dodgers in 1948. After brief stints with the New York Giants and Baltimore Orioles, he came to Detroit in 1960. The only broadcaster to be traded for a player, Ernie worked both TV and radio when he started in Detroit, but after 1965 he was heard exclusively on radio.

110

NORMAN CASH, 1960. "Stormin' Norman" rounds third and gets the hand of coach Jo-Jo White after he ripped one of his 377 career home runs. Norm was originally drafted by the NFL's Chicago Bears, but he opted to play baseball, beginning with the Chicago White Sox in 1958. He was traded to Detroit from Cleveland in 1960.

DICK BROWN. Catcher Dick Brown strides into one at Tiger Stadium. Dick came to the Tigers in 1961 after tours with the Indians and White Sox. He was a dependable catcher with occasional home run power, playing two seasons with the Bengals before being traded to Baltimore in 1963. Surgery for a brain tumor ended his career in 1965, and he died in 1970 of cancer at the age of 35.

THE TIGERS' KEYSTONE COMBO, 1961. Shortstop Chico Fernandez tries to get a handle on the ball, as second baseman Jake Wood readies to take the throw. The second base umpire looks on. Fernandez came up with the Dodgers as a bright prospect but could not displace Pee Wee Reese. The Phillies traded five players to get him in 1957. The Tigers gave him the shortstop job in

1960. In 1962 he showed some power, hitting 20 home runs. Jake Wood was among the fastest men in the American League. He led the league in triples and finished third in steals. He was traded to the Reds in 1967.

THE FAMOUS COLAVITO STRETCH. The "Rock" was acquired in a stunning trade with Cleveland, the home run champion (Colavito) for the batting champion (Kuenn), in 1960. After a year of adjustment in Detroit, Rocky had his greatest season in 1961, hitting .290 with 45 home runs and 140 runs batted in.

FEARSOME FOURSOME, 1961. Four great sluggers pose together before a game in September. Pictured from left to right are Roger Maris, Rocky Colavito, Norm Cash, and Mickey Mantle. These players helped to keep their teams in the pennant race. They accounted for 201 home runs hit in 1961. Maris broke Babe Ruth's record with 61, Colavito hit 45, Cash hit 41, and Mantle hit 54.

HOME RUN ACTION, 1961. Tiger catcher Dick Brown is greeted at home plate by the reception of players who scored before him. Brown's grand slam scored Norm Cash, Steve Boros, and Rocky Colavito in the fifth inning against the Boston Red Sox and paced the Tigers to a 9-5 victory.

BILLY BRUTON, 1961. Billy beats the throw and first baseman Steve Bilko to the bag. He broke in with the Milwaukee Braves and led the National League in stolen bases in each of his first three seasons. Billy came to Detroit in 1961 along with Dick Brown, Terry Fox, and Chuck Cottier. He was one of the finest defensive outfielders that the Tigers ever had.

A Pair of Sevens. These two sluggers and rivals were caught chatting during batting practice before a double header on the Fourth of July weekend. The Tigers and Yankees battled for the 1961 pennant right up to September, when the Yankees pitching depth showed through. The Bengals would win 101 games and finish 8 games out of first.

Tiger Action, 1962. Tiger third baseman Steve Boros slides safely into third as the Yankees Clete Boyer swings around too late for the tag. He had singled and advanced on Billy Bruton's single. Pitcher Bill Stafford (22) was chased moments later when both Tigers scored on Norm Cash's double. The Tigers managed to hold on to win 7-5.

A HIGH-RISE CATCHER, 1962. Boston Red Sox catcher Russ Nixon goes vertical to retrieve a wild throw from center field after Dick Brown's single. That is utility infielder Dick McAuliffe scoring on the play followed closely by Bob Osborne, who also came in on the error. McAuliffe hit .263 in a part-time role that season.

HIGH-FLYING ACTION, 1963. Tiger shortstop Dick McAuliffe goes high in the air after taking the throw from pitcher Jim Bunning and forcing a sliding Bobby Richardson of the New York Yankees. The season was much of a washout as the Tigers finished fifth, the manager lost his job, and the fans lost interest.

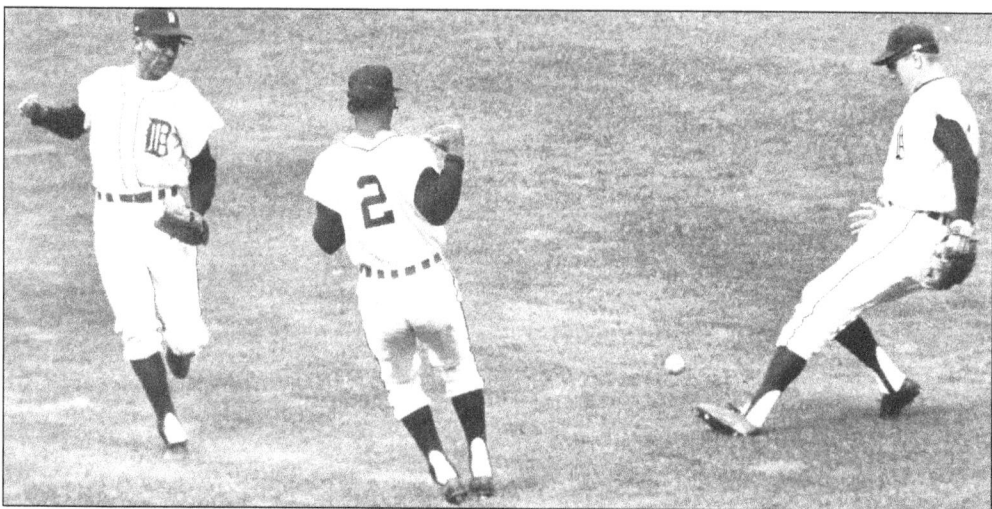

THAT KIND OF SEASON, 1963. Pictured from left to right are Billy Bruton, Jake Wood, and Al Kaline. They have the ball surrounded, but it drops in for a single anyway in a game against the Cleveland Indians in which they won 9-3. Tiger Stadium attendance dropped 400,000 to a 20-year low of 821,952 diehard fans.

A BRIGHT SPOT FOR THE FUTURE, 1963. New Tiger catcher Gus Triandos is greeted at the dugout steps by Al Kaline, Norm Cash, and others after homering against the Chicago White Sox. Triandos wasn't the only newcomer in 1963. Rookies Mickey Lolich, Bill Freehan, and Gates Brown were all learning their trade.

118

OPENING DAY, 1967. Catcher Bill Freehan prepares to take the first pitch of the 1967 season from Earl Wilson. Wilson would lead the staff and the majors with 22 wins in his first full season as a Tiger. Freehan became the league's dominant catcher with a .282 season and placed third in the voting for the most valuable player.

THE DOG DAYS OF AUGUST, 1967. The Cleveland Indians' Tony Horton looks helplessly on as Tiger shortstop Ray Oyler completes the double play to pitcher Denny McLain covering first. Oyler, an excellent glove man but not a hitter, came up to the Tigers in 1965 as a shortstop but gave up the job to Mickey Stanley in the 1968 World Series. Ray was traded to the expansion Seattle Pilots.

EARLY SEASON ACTION, 1968. First baseman Norm Cash slices one to the right field corner. Cash would hit 15 doubles and 25 home runs while platooning the first base position with Al Kaline. He would commit only eight errors while turning in a .992 fielding average to go along with a .263 batting average.

THE PINCH-HITTER AND THE COACH. Gates Brown shares a moment with Coach Pat Mullin, who worked hard to get the "Gator" into Tiger stripes. In his first major league at-bat, Brown homered as a pinch-hitter off Boston's Don Heffner at Fenway Park. He would hit 16 pinch home runs among 107 pinch hits and retire in 1975 as the premier pinch-hitter in American League history.

DENNY MCLAIN. The "Sky King" first came up to the club in 1963 and showed flashes of brilliance, winning 16 games in 1965, 20 in 1966, and 17 in 1967. But 1968 was McLain's year. He won 31 of 37 decisions—Detroit's first and only 30-game winner. He was the League MVP and unanimous Cy Young Award winner with a 1.96 ERA, 28 complete games, and 280 strikeouts.

JOHN HILLER. This Canadian save artist survived a massive stroke in 1971 and was pitching for the Tigers by the end of 1972. He started with the club in 1965 and had moderate success as a reliever and an occasional starter. On August 6, 1968, he tied a major league record for consecutive strikeouts from the start of a game with six.

TWO AMERICAN LEAGUE SLUGGERS. Detroit's own Willie Horton chats with Boston's Carl Yastremski before a game. Willie would lead the 1968 Tiger regulars with a .285 batting average and a .543 slugging average in a season that would see only one American Leaguer hit .300. Carl Yastremski would claim that honor with a .304 average.

BIG GUN WILLIE, 1968. A graduate of Northwestern High School, Willie came right to the Tigers in 1963 and hit his first home run off Robin Roberts. He became the team's left fielder in 1965, his first full major league season, and was an all-star, hitting .273 with 29 home runs and 104 runs batted in. Willie contributed 36 four-baggers to the 1968 season and in the World Series nailed Lou Brock at the plate in game five.

BIG BILL FREEHAN. Bill signed with the Tigers from the University of Michigan as a bonus baby in 1961. By 1963, he had become the regular catcher, a position he would hold for 14 seasons. One year later he had his first and only season as a .300 hitter and made his first of ten straight All-Star appearances.

PREMIER CATCHER. Not only an offensive threat, Bill Freehan was one of the American League's dominant defensive back-stoppers as well. He won five Gold Gloves in his career, and in 1965 he tied the record for putouts in a game with 19. In 1968, he set an American League record for most putouts (971) and chances in a year.

COMPLETE THE DOUBLE PLAY. Second baseman Dick McAuliffe turns and fires to first base to complete one of 79 double plays in 1968. During that season, he had 288 putouts and 348 assists while committing only 9 errors for a .986 fielding average. He was also one of the best lead-off men of his era and went the entire season without hitting into a double play.

MITCHELL JACK STANLEY. "Mickey" Stanley, a native of Grand Rapids, spent his entire 15-year major league career with Detroit, starting in 1964. He was an outstanding defensive center fielder, winning four Gold Gloves and having a 1.000 fielding average in 1968. In order to get Al Kaline's bat into the World Series line up, Mayo Smith moved Mickey Stanley to shortstop, a gamble that paid off.

LOCKER ROOM PEP TALK. Manager Mayo Smith addresses his troops in the locker room prior to the game. A minor league outfielder for more than 20 seasons, Smith became the Phillies manager in 1955 and was hired by the Tigers in 1967. Losing the pennant on the last day in 1967, he took the Bengals all the way in 1968.

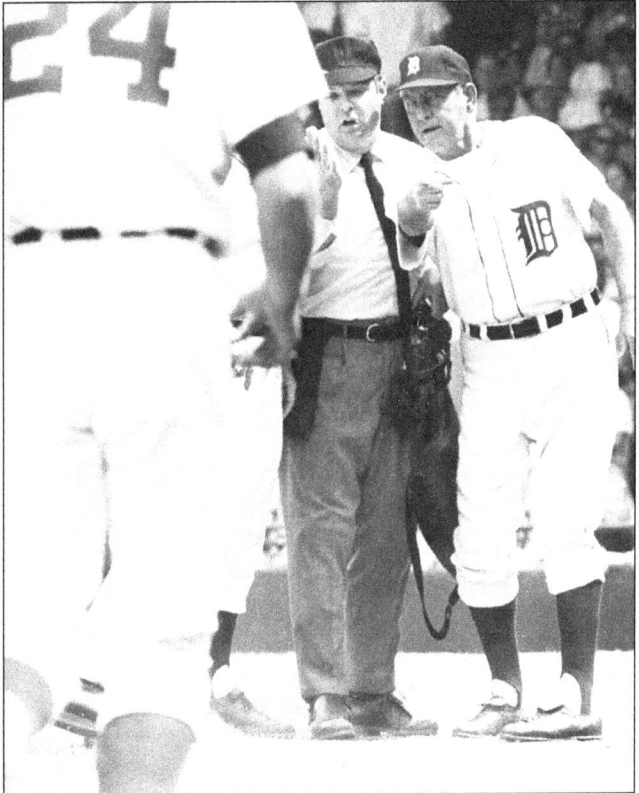

A PHILOSOPHICAL DISCUSSION. Making sure the umpire is making the correct call, Mayo Smith points out the error of his way in this rather calm discussion during the 1968 campaign. Smith was once thrown out of a game in the tunnel going to the dugout before the teams took the field. He asked the umpire if they were going to play that game according to the rules.

MICKEY LOLICH. Portly Mickey Lolich came up to the Tigers from Portland, Oregon, in 1963 and stayed through the 1975 season. He broke his left collarbone as a child and rehabilitation made his left arm stronger than his right. He is probably the best left-handed pitcher the Tigers ever had and was much more consistent than Denny McLain, who came up in the same year.

BATTERY MATE CHAMPIONS. Bill Freehan walks out to congratulate his partner, Mickey Lolich, after a successful afternoon outing. Despite Denny McLain's 31-win season, Lolich would steal the spotlight with three World Series victories, giving up only five runs in his three complete games. He posted an earned run average of 1.67 with 21 strikeouts.

THE HOME RUN TROT, 1968.
Right fielder Al Kaline displays his home-run trot after hitting his second World Series round-tripper. After a 24-year wait, Al would finally get to participate in postseason play. He batted a hefty .379, the best on the team, with two home runs and eight runs batted in.

WORLD SERIES FEVER, 1968.
The Brass Rail Bar on Lafayette Boulevard borrows a cereal slogan to celebrate the championship. The Tigers completed a rare and remarkable comeback, down three games to one, to defeat the defending champion St. Louis Cardinals. In a classic game seven pitchers' duel, the Bengals finally broke through in the seventh inning with three runs and held on to become the last real champions of baseball.

ALL-TIME TIGER TEAM. This composite photograph shows the elected members of the All-Time Tiger Team for the first 50 years of their participation in the American League. They are, from left to right, as follows: manager, Hugh Jennings; pitchers, Schoolboy Rowe, Tommy Bridges, George Mullin, Bill Donovan, and Hal Newhouser; catcher, Mickey Cochrane; outfield, Ty Cobb, Sam Crawford, and Harry Heilman; first base, Hank Greenberg; second base, Charlie Gehringer; third base, George Kell; and shortstop, Donie Bush. As this century comes to a close, we must hold another election to claim the Tiger greats from the second 50 years.

www.ingramcontent.com/pod-product-compliance
Lightning Source LLC
Chambersburg PA
CBHW050922150426
42812CB00051B/1968